# Charles Dickens

Peter Leigh

Published in association with The Basic Skills Agency

## Hodder & Stoughton

A MEMBER OF THE HODDER HEADLINE GROUP

## Acknowledgements

Cover: Portrait of Charles Dickens by William Powell Frith (1819–1909), Victoria & Albert Museum, London, UK/Bridgeman Art Library

Photos: pp iv, 4, 11,14, 22 Mary Evans Picture Library; p 17 Popperfoto

Every effort has been made to trace copyright holders of material reproduced in this book. Any rights not acknowledged will be acknowledged in subsequent printings if notice is given to the publisher.

Orders; please contact Bookpoint Ltd, 39 Milton Park, Abingdon, Oxon OX14 4TD. Telephone: (44) 01235 400414, Fax: (44) 01235 400454. Lines are open from 9.00–6.00, Monday to Saturday, with a 24 hour message answering service.
Email address: orders@bookpoint.co.uk

*British Library Cataloguing in Publication Data*
A catalogue record for this title is available from the British Library

ISBN  0 340 77655 2

First published  2000
Impression number   10 9 8 7 6 5 4 3 2 1
Year                2005 2004 2003 2002 2001 2000

Copyright © 2000

Typeset by GreenGate Publishing Services, Tonbridge, Kent.
Printed in Great Britain for Hodder and Stoughton Educational, a division of Hodder Headline Plc, 338 Euston Road, London NW1 3BH, by Redwood Books, Trowbridge, Wilts

# Contents

# 1 Childhood

Charles Dickens was born in 1812.
By the age of twelve his life was in ruins.
His father had gone to prison.
He had to support his mother and sister.

He was taken away from school,
and set to work in a factory.
It was a 'blacking' factory.
It made boot polish
and a special black coating for iron stoves.

He worked there for twelve hours a day.
It was child slavery.
As he could read and write
he was given a job as a clerk.
He sat at a desk next to a window.
The other children had to work
in the fumes from the tubs of hot blacking.

The factory was by the river in London.
In those days the river was an open sewer.
The factory was damp, rotten, and filthy.
It was only held up above the mud
by the buildings on either side of it.
Thousands of people lived and worked
in sheds like this.
Thousands died too.

Dickens lived a long way from the factory
in lodgings.
After work he would buy a penny loaf
and tramp all the way across London
to his room.
There he would sit and eat the loaf.
It was all he could afford.
He was cold, lonely, and frightened.

Once a week he went to see his father.
His father was in prison for debt.
In those days you went to prison for that.
They even had a special prison for it
Once you were in, that was it.
You had no way of paying off your debt.
People spent years there, died there,
even if the debt was tiny.

It was not like other prisons.
Whole families lived there.
People could come and go,
except the prisoners of course.
There weren't any cells,
just dark, dirty rooms.
A family did everything there –
cook, eat, sleep, and wash.
There was no running water –
just one well for the whole prison.

As he walked to and from the factory
and the prison,
Dickens got to know every bit of London.
Not just the fine houses and broad streets
of the rich, but also the slums and dark alleys
of the poor.
He also got to know the underworld –
the pickpockets and muggers,
the beggars, and the gangs of children
who lived by robbing.
He knew how they worked, where they lived,
and the words they used.

Dickens took it all in.
His bright, dark eyes soaked it all up.

Marshalsea Prison, 1804.

His father wasn't in prison for long.
He was left a little money by a relative.
It was just enough to get him out.
Dickens was lucky.
He left the factory and came back home.
He went to school again.
Everything seemed fine.
To his family he was the same cheerful boy.

But he never forgot this time.
He had seen the dark side of London.
It haunted him and gave him nightmares.
It lies behind all his work.

## 2  The Storyteller

While he was in the factory,
Dickens began to tell stories.
At first he told them just to himself –
to escape, or to amuse himself.
Then he began to tell them
to the others at the factory.
The ragged children would gather round
and listen keenly.
It was the only escape they had.

He began to use his talent as a storyteller.
Even at this young age he was a master.
He was a wonderful mimic, and
had an amazing eye for detail.
He could describe something
and make it come alive –
even everyday things.
This was Dickens' greatest gift,
and one that he was never to lose.

As he grew into a young man
he tried several jobs.
He didn't stay in any of them for very long.
He was unsettled.
He did not get on with his parents,
and he blamed them for what had happened to him.
His father could not be trusted with money.
His mother had betrayed him
by sending him to the blacking factory.
He was right about his father –
many years later he caught him
forging his name on cheques.
He was unfair to his mother.
What else could she have done?
Honest work for women
was very difficult in those days
and she had a family to think of.

However Dickens held this against his mother
for the rest of his life,
Perhaps he held it against other women, too.
He never had easy relationships with women.
In his mind women were
either angels or monsters.

There was a pattern in his life
that he repeated several times
He would meet an eighteen-year-old girl
and fall hopelessly in love with her.
He would idolise her,
and make her into a saint.
Then as soon as he knew her better,
or she got older, or married someone
then he would lose interest in her.

The first of these eighteen-year-olds
was a girl called Mary Beadnell.
She was young and pretty,
the daughter of a banker,
She liked Dickens
because he was an attractive young man.
He was also small, with intense black eyes.
He was also very good company.
He kept people amused for hours
with his stories.
Much as Mary liked Dickens,
she did not want him as a lover.
Dickens was very upset.
For years he had special feelings for her.

Many years later when they were both
middle-aged, Mary wrote to Dickens
and asked if they could meet again.
He was a famous author by now
but in his mind she was still
young and beautiful.
In fact she was tubby, empty-headed,
and gossiped the whole time.
Dickens was very disappointed –
but it shows what an unreal picture
he always had of women.

When he first met Mary
Dickens had hardly begun to write.
The idea came to him
only after he became a reporter.
He had to listen very carefully
to all the speeches in Parliament.
Then he had to write down exactly
what was being said.

Dickens was very good at it.
He began to think
if he could write this,
then why not stories of his own?

At that time magazines with pictures
were very popular.
The pictures were like big cartoons.
A story would go with the cartoon.
Dickens wrote a funny story
which he thought would be right for a magazine.
Although he was very shy, late one night,
with fear and trembling as he later said,
he dropped it in the post box.
Later that month
when he went to buy a copy of the magazine,
he found his story had been printed.

It was one of the happiest
and proudest moments of his life.
He said 'my eyes were so dimmed
with joy and pride
that they could not bear the street.'

Dickens's career as a writer had started.

# 3  The Road to Success

Dickens published eight more stories
in the magazine.
Then, when he was twenty four
he had his first break.

A publisher wanted to put
all his writings together
and publish them with pictures.
In fact, the publisher wanted the pictures
more than he wanted Dickens's writing.
The writing was just an excuse
for the pictures – it was the pictures that sold the
magazines.

That didn't worry Dickens.
Soon all his writings and several pictures
were published under the title
*Sketches by Boz.*

It was a great success.
Two weeks after it first appeared
the publisher asked Dickens
if he would write some more.

Dickens agreed but said he wanted to link
the pieces together in one long story.

The publisher was unsure.
Such a thing had never been done before.
Dickens had his way.
In 1836 the first copy of
*The Pickwick Papers* was published.

It was more than a success.
It was a sensation –
even by today's standards.
They started by printing 400 copies.
By the end of the month
they had to print 40,000!
Dickens had become the most popular writer
of the day.

He had also invented something new –
the serial.
Instead of one long book,
the story is split up into parts.
One part comes out each month.
The reader gets hooked on the first one,
and buys the second to see what happens.
It's a bit similar to the TV soaps of today.

Dickens wrote all his novels like this.
In fact he wrote only one month ahead.
He often didn't know the end of the story,
until half of it was already printed.

They were all very popular,
in the same way as TV soaps are today.
People used to talk about the characters
as if they were real.
When Little Nell was dying in
*The Old Curiosity Shop*,
the whole country went into mourning.
People felt as if their own child was dying.
It wasn't only in this country,
but world-wide too.
As the boats from England
pulled into New York,
people shouted from the shore:
'Is Little Nell dead yet?'

If readers thought Dickens's characters
were real it was because Dickens did so too!
He often said that his characters would do
what they wanted to do,
and not what he wanted them to do.

Working conditions in factories in the 1800s were terrible –
especially for children.

Dickens's first novel was a comedy –
but soon his darker side began to show.
Even before he had finished
*The Pickwick Papers*
he had begun *Oliver Twist*.
He used all that he had seen
in the London underworld
when he had worked in the factory.

People were shocked by
the story of the poor orphan Oliver –
the boy who dared to ask for more.
It touched their hearts.

It showed them things
they didn't want to know about –
the crime, the dirt, how poor people really lived.
For the first time Dickens showed
the power of his imagination.

His writing really did have an effect.
He made people want to change things.
During his lifetime London was cleaned up.
The slums were cleared
and proper drains were laid.

Dickens showed the power of his work
in his public readings.
These were great events.
Thousands came to hear him.

They took place in large halls or theatres.
Every seat would be taken.
The stage would be bare
apart from a reading desk and lamp.
He would look around the hall
with his deep black eyes,
and he would begin to read.
Then the magic began.
He used all the skills he had learnt
in the blacking factory.
He made the stories so alive to the audience
that it was as if they were watching a film.
He acted out all the parts,
and gave each character its own voice.
The people really seemed to see
the story in front of them.

So Dickens became
not only the most popular writer of his day,
but also the most popular entertainer.

No one knew until many years later,
the cost of this to Dickens himself.

Charles Dickens was a popular entertainer.

# 4  Married Life

All his success had not made Dickens happy.

He had married at the beginning of his career
to a girl named Catherine Hogarth.
When she first met him, he had little money.
By the time he married her
he was a rich and famous author.
It didn't change her feelings –
it was Dickens that had the problem.
It was the same problem as before.
Catherine seemed a beautiful girl
when he first met her
He adored her.
As soon as he married her,
he lost interest.
He thought she was dull –
she bored him.
Despite this she loved him dearly
throughout her life.

They had ten children.
All of them say the same thing
about their father –
when they were young, he was wonderful.
They had all sorts of treats and surprises.
As they grew older,
he seemed to lose interest in them.
When they were grown-up
he was cold towards them.
As one of his sons said,
'It is not easy being the son of a genius.'

Catherine had two sisters.
In many ways they were closer to Dickens
than Catherine herself.
In fact the eldest, Georgina,
took over the running of the house.
Catherine was never very good
at managing things,
especially as the wife of a famous author.

Catherine's younger sister, Mary,
died when she was only seventeen.
Everyone in the family was deeply upset,
especially Dickens.

He wore her ring, and kept a lock of her hair
next to his heart.
He dreamt about her every night.
He kept all her clothes.
Every few days he would take them out.
He had 'Young, beautiful and good'
written on her gravestone.
He said he wanted to be buried with her.

She was another of his perfect girls.
This must have been very difficult
for Catherine, especially since she, too,
was very upset by her sister's death.

To the outside world, they were a happy family
but as Dickens reached middle age, he changed.
The dark side of his imagination
seemed to overcome him.
He would walk for hours by himself,
lost in his own world.

He seemed much older than he was.
He also started behaving oddly –
he would suddenly quarrel with old friends,
people he had known for years.
He would be bright one minute, his old self,
and then suddenly fall into black depression.

His writing became much darker too.
There was little comedy or lightness
in the stories he wrote at this time.

No one knows why Dickens became like this.
It just seems that the strain of writing
those wonderful stories and all his public readings
became too much for him.
Then suddenly he and Catherine separated.
Catherine did not want to –
it was Dickens who wanted it.
In those days husbands held
a lot of power over their wives.
He also wanted the children to stay with him.
He would not let them see their mother very often.

He got very angry if they talked about her.
He wouldn't even let her come
to their daughter's wedding.
This was very hard on Catherine,
and on the children.
However, she remained loyal to him
to the end.
She always said she loved him
and wanted him back
till the day of his death.

Charles Dickens at his home in Gadshill with his daughters.

A separation was a much bigger thing then
than it is today.
Dickens tried to keep it quiet
but as the news got out people were shocked.

He had written such wonderful, warm stories
of families and childhood.
People had taken him to their hearts.
When people found out how badly
he had treated Catherine,
they began to like and read him less.
He wrote to the papers
and tried to explain himself
but that was a mistake.
What made it even worse
was a news story that he had left Catherine
for an eighteen-year-old actress.

It was true.
Or at least partly true.
She was Ellen Ternan.
She always said that
she and Dickens were never lovers.
She said there was nothing wrong
with their friendship.
She was another young woman
who became an idol for Dickens.
He didn't want to touch her.
He wanted to keep her pure
in his imagination.

But other people thought they were lovers.
The more they denied it
the more people thought it was true.
Dickens was very hurt by all of this.
He hated people thinking badly of him.
It was another cause of the pain
that aged him in these years.

# 5  The Last Years

One afternoon Dickens was travelling
to London on a train.
He was with Ellen Ternan and her mother.
As they were going over a bridge,
the train suddenly came off the rails.
Several carriages crashed into the river below.
The carriage Dickens was in was saved,
but was left hanging over the edge.

Ellen screamed,
but Dickens remained calm.
He managed to open a door
and get Ellen and her mother out safely.

Then he heard the screams from the people
in the carriages in the river below.
He climbed down the bank,
and for the next few hours
did everything he could for the injured
and the dying.
He rescued some from the wreckage
and brought water and blankets to others.

Many said later they owed their lives to him, and all
remembered the words of comfort
he brought to the dying.
When there was nothing more he could do,
he got on another train
and went to London

When he got back home,
the shock hit him.
For the next few days
he could hardly walk or talk.
His friends were shocked at how shaken he was.
He seemed suddenly to be an old man.
His nerves were never the same again.

Even two years later
he could suddenly be overcome with terror.
He would grip the arms of his chair.
Sweat would run down his face,
as he stared blankly into space.
It was as if he was seeing
the same awful scenes, again.
Like before, he was overcome
by the terrible power of his imagination.

A few years later,
Dickens went on a reading tour of America.
Friends told him not to – he was too weak
but his mind was made up.
He also insisted on reading *Sikes and Nancy.*
He was clear, too, that he wanted to read
the scene of Nancy's murder.
It was always one of the most exciting parts
of his readings.

Night after night Dickens performed it.
He gave it everything he had.
People who heard him
remembered it for years after.
As Nancy is clubbed to death by Bill Sikes,
Dickens seemed to be Nancy.
As Bill Sikes is driven mad,
Dickens seemed to be him.
It was both wonderful and terrible.

When he returned to England
he was exhausted.
He did do some more performances,
but he was sinking fast.

One day he collapsed while out walking
and was rushed home.
Ellen was called to his bedside.
He never recovered and
died the next day.
He was fifty eight years old.

His funeral was held a few days later.
All his friends and family were there,
and all the famous people of the day.
There was just one person absent.
Catherine was not asked.

When a popular writer dies
people often lose interest in their work.
This was never true of Dickens.
All his books are still in print.
They are in every language.
They have all been filmed several times.
He is still one of the most popular
writers in the world.